Bear Grounds Coffee Co.

501(c)3 registered nonprofit organization.
EIN: 93-2614362
All donations are tax deductible.
beargroundscoffee.org
All profits on this book go toward conserving bears and their habitats worldwide.

This Book Belongs to...

Copyright © 2024 by Bear Grounds Coffee Co. All Rights Reserved.
No part of this book may be reproduced or used in any matter without written permission of the copvright owner except for the use of quotations in a book review.
For more information, address: info@beargroundscoffee.org

All About Bears

Illustrated & Written By: Jessica Berry

Dedication

To all bears across the globe, the wonderful Bear Grounds Coffee Co. team, and the youth who will be inspired to care for the Earth.

Welcome to the wonderful world of bears.

Did you know that bears are some of the coolest creatures in the wild?

Let's explore together and learn all about them.

Meet the bear family.

There are 8 different species of bears.

Check out this handy map during your journey to see where each bear is from.

The Bear Grounds of the World:

Legend:

- 🔴 Polar Bear
- 🟤 Grizzly/Brown Bear
- ⚫ Black Bear
- 🔵 Speckled Bear
- ⚫ Asian Black Bear
- 🔵 Sloth Bear
- 🟢 Sun Bear
- 🟣 Panda Bear

Hi, my name is Talia the <u>Polar Bear.</u> I live in the cold Arctic.

I love spending my time fishing or being in the water. In fact - I spend SO much time in the water that I'm considered a MARINE mammal.

Some of my favorite snacks are seals and arctic foxes.

Hi! My name is Sunny the <u>Sun Bear</u>.

I live in the forests of South East Asia. I am the smallest bear species. I only stand four to five feet tall, making me smaller than the average human.

I avoid people so a lot of my behavior is a mystery.

I am Marceline the Black Bear. I live in American forests and mountains. I love to eat fruit, grass, and sometimes fish!

Out of all the bears, I am the most common. I can even have 6 cubs in one litter.

I live closer to humans than other bears.

Did you know I can be white, black, cinnamon, gray or blonde?

I am Paco the <u>Grizzly Bear</u>. I can be found in Canada, Alaska, and some northern American states.

I am an Apex predator – which means no other animals are above me on the food chain! My front claws can get up to four inches long. I like to play wrestle with my bear friends.

I LOVE salmon and can eat up to 30 pounds of food in one day.

Hello, I am a <u>Sloth Bear.</u> Be very still, I am trying to catch my next snack. I love termites and ants.

My nostrils can close completely. This protects me from breathing in dust when I'm hunting for insects.

If you want to find me, I live in forests and grasslands in Sri Lanka, India, and Nepal.

I am Alice the <u>Asian Black Bear</u>. Some people like to call me a Moon Bear. I live in the forests and mountains of Asia and can live up to 25 years in the wild!

I love to climb, but in old age sometimes I can be too heavy to do so. Ugh!

I munch on a lot of stuff. I eat all kinds of things from berries to birds.

Hi, I am Polly the <u>Panda Bear</u>. I am from China. My favorite foods are bamboo and leaves. Because I am a vegetarian, I don't get enough fuel to hibernate like my other bear friends. This is why I have camouflage that doubles as communication! My colors help me blend in with my snowy and shadowy environment.

My dark ears signal my intent of ferocity and my eye markings help other pandas know who I am.

I'm Larry the <u>Spectacled Bear</u>. I am sitting on a bear claw pastry. I am an omnivore, which means I eat a bit of everything.

I live in the Andes Mountains and South America. My species evolved from the extinct short-faced bear.

I am the 3rd heaviest land mammal in South America.

Bears have big appetites. Depending on the species, their diets vary from bamboo to meat. Can you find each bear on the map and their diet?

To find their meals, they have a good sense of smell. In fact, it is their strongest sense. They can smell food 18 to 20 miles away.

Look at this Tibetan Blue Bear, the rarest-sighted bear, sniffing out some grub.

Did you know bears can run, swim, and even climb trees? They're super talented athletes. They can also be very lazy when some of us hibernate for the Winter.

They look cuddly and cute, but they would like it if you stayed away. They have little desire to interact with humans, unless they are forced to, or they are near a food source. You know, like a trash can.

Bear homes are getting lost and destroyed due to logging, oil drilling, mining, and land development. Out of the eight kinds of bears, six of them are endangered.

Due to the destructive ways we harvest the Earth's energy resources, many bear dens are destroyed and ice is melted.

We can create a happier place to live for all species through renewable energy and not disrupting animal habitats.

If you see a bear in real life, keep your distance and tell your mom or dad. Do not hurt the bear. If you do then its family will be sad.

Bears have a critical, invisible space around them. Once something gets in that space, they feel the need to act! They can either run away or get aggressive. Depending on which bear you meet, the way they react can vary.

We've had a bear-y good time learning All About Bears with you. But don't worry, there's always more to discover in the wild. In fact, there are even more kinds of bears to learn about.

Stay curious and kind to the Earth! There is so much to explore on our planet. Mysteries are just waiting for you to uncover them!

Until next time, friend.

www.ingramcontent.com/pod-product-compliance
Ingram Content Group UK Ltd.
Pitfield, Milton Keynes, MK11 3LW, UK
UKHW050656080725
6779UKWH00035B/434